MOUNTAIN BIKES

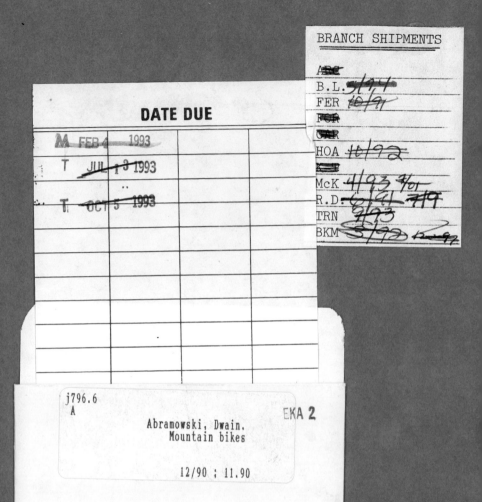

MOUNTAIN BIKES

BY DWAIN ABRAMOWSKI

Franklin Watts
New York London Toronto Sydney
A First Book 1990

Library of Congress Cataloging-in-Publication Data

Abramowski, Dwain.
Mountain bikes / Dwain Abramowski.
p.   cm.—(First book)
Includes bibliographical references.
Summary: Discusses the techniques, preparations, safety
precautions, and equipment necessary for using mountain bikes.
ISBN 0-531-10871-6
1. All terrain cycling—Juvenile literature.   2. All terrain
bicycles—Juvenile literature.   [1. All terrain bicycles.   2. All
terrain cycling.]   I. Title.   II. Series.
GV1056.A27   1990
796.6—dc20   90-31879   CIP   AC

Cover photograph courtesy
of Gamma-Liaison

Other photographs
courtesy of Dwain Abramowski, except
frontis and p. 8, courtesy
of Dave Black

CONTENTS

Thanks to my wife Chris and my son Nathan for their love and support.

WHAT IS
A MOUNTAIN BIKE?

A mountain bike or, as it is sometimes called, an All-Terrain Bike (ATB) is different from other bicycles. It has special features and equipment that allow it to go down gravel roads, through wooded trails, and up and down mountains. A mountain bike rider can compete in races and play mountain bike games, or just use it to ride to school and around the neighborhood.

Mountain bike tires are very wide and the tread is very deep. Some mountain bike tires have tread patterns that look like the tread on farm tractor tires.

Mountain bikes also have fifteen, eighteen, or twenty-one speeds. Many mountain bikes have "click" shifting. This allows the rider to change gears quickly, without pushing the shifter too far or too fast and missing a gear. To make shifting easier and quicker, the shifters are mounted on the handlebars within easy reach of the riders' thumbs. Some shifting systems even allow the rider to shift while climbing hills or making fast turns without "grinding" the gears.

The handlebars on a mountain bike are more upright than those on a regular ten-speed bike (also known as a road-bike), but not as high as a BMX-style bike. Mountain bike handlebars are usually straight or slightly curved back toward the rider. Mountain bikes are made from a variety of metals: steel, chrome-molybdenum tubing (known as chromoly), aluminum, titanium (a material that is commonly used to make things that need to be light and strong, such as jets), or carbon fiber. Mountain bikes can also be made from a combination of these materials, making the bike light and strong.

HISTORY OF MOUNTAIN BIKES

Mountain biking started in Marin County, in northern California, during the late 1970s. The first races took place on the steep fire road that wound down Mount Tamalpais in Marin County. Early mountain bikes had coaster brakes, and because the course was so steep most riders used their brakes all the way down. This would cause the grease in the coaster brakes to get very hot and

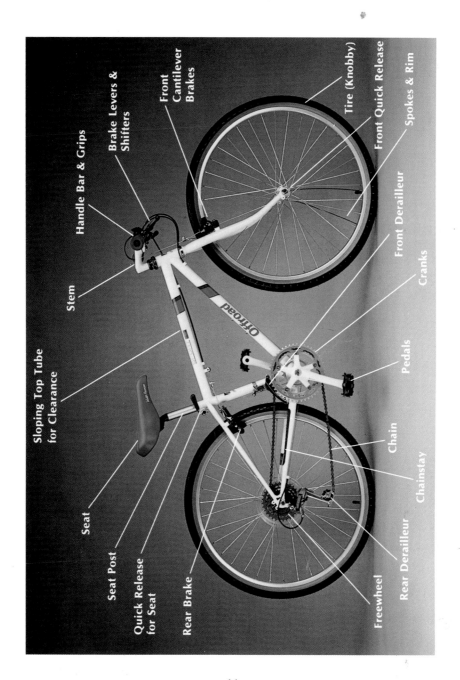

Sloping Top Tube for Clearance

Handle Bar & Grips

Brake Levers & Shifters

Front Cantilever Brakes

Tire (Knobby)

Front Quick Release

Spokes & Rim

Stem

Front Derailleur

Cranks

Pedals

Seat

Chain

Chainstay

Seat Post

Quick Release for Seat

Rear Brake

Freewheel

Rear Derailleur

begin to smoke. By the end of a race the brake had burned up all the grease and needed to be "repacked" with new grease before the bike could be safely ridden again. Because of this, they named the fire road "Repack."

Early bikes were usually something the rider had put together, because there was nothing available at the bicycle shop. The first mountain bikes were not much more than old, sturdy touring bikes, called "clunkers" because they were sometimes rusty and looked rather worn out. They were also very heavy. Some of the first bikes weighed as much as fifty pounds. These clunkers were fitted with the widest tires that the rider could find. Some had five or ten speeds. Many early mountain bikes had drum brakes (on the front and rear tires), and motorcycle brake levers. Some bikes had moto-cross (motorcycle) handlebars.

The bikers who built and rode their bikes down "Repack" learned a lot about what an off-road bike had to be able to do. Joe Breeze, Tom Ritchey, Steve Potts, Charlie Cunningham, and Gary Fisher were the first mountain bike frame designers and builders. The mountain bikes that are out on the trails today were influenced by these mountain bike builders back in the late 1970s and early 1980s.

RIDING A MOUNTAIN BIKE

Riding a mountain bike, especially in the woods and on hills and mountains, is very different from riding on the sidewalk or street. You must be a good bike rider before you attempt to ride off-road. Learning to control the bike is very important. Make sure you are able to start, turn, and stop when necessary in order to avoid hitting obstacles and keep your speed down.

As with any activity, caution and experience is most important. Mountain biking is potentially dangerous. Do not ride beyond your capabilities. Always wear a helmet, preserve nature, watch for others on the trail, and wear appropriate safety attire.

SHIFTING—BRAKING— PEDALING

Shifting a mountain bike is similar to shifting a ten-speed. Mountain bike shifting systems are mounted on the handlebars so that you can maintain steering control in rough terrain as you shift.

You shift in the same way you would when riding a ten-speed: a high gear for going fast and a

**The large front chainrings are
for pedaling on flat terrain.**

low gear to get more power. Mountain bikes have two or three front **chainrings,** and the **freewheel** (on the back wheel) will have five, six, or seven sprockets. Put your chain on a large front chainring and small freewheel sprocket when you are not climbing a hill and want to get as much speed as possible. Shift to a low gear, or small chainring, in the front and a large one in the back to get power each time you pedal. On the trails you will often find you are riding on the middle chainring. Use the higher gears to ride on the roads and the lower gears to climb hills and go through sand or mud.

Brake levers are mounted right next to the shift levers. Often the levers themselves are shorter than road-bike levers. They are sometimes called **shorty levers** (or two-finger levers). Because they are shorter than road levers, there is less chance of catching them on a branch or bush as you go down a trail.

When braking it is best to be prepared. Plan ahead so that you can apply your brakes with a steady pressure, rather than locking them up. If you apply the front brake only—and do it too fast— you can lift the back end of the bike in the air and even find yourself going over the handlebars. Though there is no risk of going over the handle-

The small front chainring and large
rear freewheel sprocket are used when
the terrain is steep or when the trail
becomes muddy, sandy, or rough.

When you apply your brakes, use both the
front and back brake to avoid being pitched
over the bars or having the back end of
the bike slide away from you.

bars by applying the back brakes hard, the rear end of the bike can still slide away from you. The back brake usually does not have as much power as the front brake.

When you pedal a mountain bike it is best to find a gear that will allow you to keep an even, steady pace. Though some chainrings are oval or egg shaped, it is still best to move the feet as if they were going in complete circles. Some pedals have **foot straps** or cages to help hold the feet secure and keep them from sliding off when pedaling hard.

CLIMBING HILLS AND MOUNTAINS

One of the first obstacles you may encounter when you ride your mountain bike is a hill. If you are not prepared, you may lose traction and stop. A good practice hill is one that is not too steep or too bumpy. When you approach the hill make sure you shift into a low gear. Sit on your seat just as you would on a bike going up a paved hill. Steer around lose gravel, rocks, potholes, and roots. Keep your speed up so that you do not lose your balance or veer off the trail.

Some hills are so steep that the only way up is to climb off your bike and hike!

On steep, rough hills it is important to be able to stand up and pedal your mountain bike. The trick to riding your mountain bike up steep hills is standing forward just enough to use all your strength, but not too far so that you lose traction and stop. It will take practice to position your body "just right." Keep enough weight on the back wheel for traction, then stand up so that you can use all the strength in your legs to pedal the bike. Standing up and pedaling also helps your bike bounce over obstacles as you climb. However, if you lean too far forward as you pedal, your back wheel will spin. You may lose traction and come to a stop.

If you don't make it up a steep hill the first time, try again with a slightly different body position as you stand over the bike. If you get tired, don't be afraid to get off your mountain bike and walk. In time, and with practice, you will be amazed at the hills you will be able to climb. There is also another side to climbing hills, the fun of going back down!

GOING DOWN MOUNTAINS!

Going down a mountainside is one of the most exciting—and one of the most difficult—things to do on a mountain bike.

Before you go down a hill or mountain make sure your mountain bike is in good working order. Your brakes should be tuned and working properly and all the bike connections must be secure: cables, levers, **derailleurs.** The right size frame is very important for going down a hill safely. A mountain bike frame should be sized a little smaller than a road-riding frame. You should have about three inches of **stand-over height** on your mountain bike. Your frame should be equipped with a **quick release** on your seat post so you can easily raise and lower your seat. If your bike is not equipped with a quick release seat, this accessory can be purchased from a mountain bike dealer. When you descend, open the quick release and push the seat down. Your seat should be narrow, so that you can extend your legs and get out over the back tire without bumping into the seat with your thighs.

Start learning how to descend hills by gradually increasing the size and length of the hills and

**You should be able to stand over the top
tube of your bike without touching it.**

mountainsides you go down. When starting off, go slow and keep your speed under control at all times. When you go down a hill on a bike, your body weight is put on the front wheel. The steeper the hill the more weight your front wheel will have and the more the bike will want to dig into the ground. Digging into the ground will make it harder to steer and control the bike. To take the weight off the front end of your bike and make it easier to steer, extend your legs a little and push your body out over the back wheel. The steeper the hill the farther out over the back wheel your body should be.

As your skill and speed increase going down the trail you will steer with the back wheel as well as the front wheel. By engaging the back brake and leaning the upper body slightly, you can turn the bike sideways toward the direction of travel. This technique is similar to a slide stop done in BMX riding, and is easier to do on loose gravel or dirt. This will take lots of practice. You may be able to learn the maneuver more easily by watching someone else do it. Any time you are riding on unfamiliar hills or trails, it is important to control your speed. Whether on a new trail or one you have been on before, always be prepared for changes in the trail and sharp dropoffs.

When going down hills it is important to keep your weight off the front tire by moving back over the rear tire.

EQUIPMENT

A mountain biker must be prepared for a variety of conditions when out on the trail. The use of proper clothing is important. There are clothes and equipment made especially for mountain biking.

To enjoy mountain biking there are really only three things you will need to ride: a helmet, eye protection (glasses or goggles), and bicycling gloves.

Off-road riding has many more hazards than road riding. A helmet will help protect your head from injury if you fall or bump an overhanging branch. Wearing eye protection will help you avoid getting sand, dust, tree limbs, and mud in your eyes. Gloves help you maintain a better grip on the handlebars when the terrain gets rough and keep your hands from tiring too fast.

Mountain biking shoes have a stiff inner sole just like the "touring shoes" that other bicyclists wear. In addition, the mountain biking shoe may have a "hiking" shoe tread. This helps a mountain biker when he or she must get off the bike and climb up rugged terrain or cross areas that may be too difficult to ride. There are also insulated shoes made for winter riding. Many mountain biking shoes have reinforced toes that fit into

Left: wearing a helmet is a must when
riding a mountain bike.
Above: toe clips help keep your feet on the pedals.

"toe clips" on the pedals. Some mountain biking shoes are make to "clip on" to a pedal. They are similar to the shoes that a ten-speed bicyclist may wear while riding on the road, but they are usually made to come out of the clip more easily. This helps when you are mountain biking, because you are much more likely to "bail out," or put your foot down to catch your balance, in rough terrain.

Mountain biking shorts and shirts are similar to the clothes other bicyclists wear, but are usually made out of more durable materials to resist tearing if snagged on a tree limb or scraped against a rock. Mountain biking shorts are also made with hip pads. Some mountain biking shirts have pads, too. Shirts with big pockets in the back are great for carrying supplies and tools. Mountain bikers should also wear knee and elbow pads if they know that the terrain is going to be rough.

CARING FOR YOUR MOUNTAIN BIKE

Unlike any other bike, a mountain bike is made to ride off-road. When out on the trail you and your mountain bike may encounter sand, mud,

Although a mountain bike is built to
handle many different trail conditions, it still
needs proper care or it can break down.

rocks, water, potholes, sticks, and gravel. A mountain bike is built to ride in these conditions, but without proper care, it can break down. There are steps you can take to prevent a breakdown.

Before you begin any ride it is important to check your bike over to make sure everything is in working order.

If you are going for a long ride, it is also wise to take some tools with you, once you know how to use them. In case of a flat tire or minor break-down, the right tools can help you ride, instead of walk, home. Tools that are handy to have include:

1. a spare tube or tube patching kit
2. a plastic tire iron and tire pump
3. a set of allen wrenches—4, 5, and 6mm
4. a small set of sockets and/or wrenches
5. a chain tool and a spoke wrench

These tools usually fit into a backpack. Or you can use a pack that fits around your waist, some-times called a "fanny" pack. There are packs that fit under your seat, or on your bike where the seat tube and the top tube of the bike meet. Packs that fit on the tubes of your bike often have a

When checking over your mountain bike:

1. Make sure the brakes work and the brake pads are centered on the rim of your tire.
2. Using a tire pressure gauge, make sure the tires have the correct amount of air in them. If they are too soft, your tube can get pinched between the rim and the tire, causing a puncture. If the pressure is too high, it may damage the bike or the bike may be hard to handle. The sidewall of the tire will usually be labeled with the correct tire pressure range(s).
3. Make sure that there are no cracks or bends in the frame of the bike. If there are, wait until it is fixed before you ride. Cracks or bends could cause the bike to break while you are out on the trail.
4. Put plenty of lubricant on your chain, then wipe it dry so that it doesn't collect a lot of sand and dirt.
5. Be sure the derailleurs are lubricated and shifting properly.

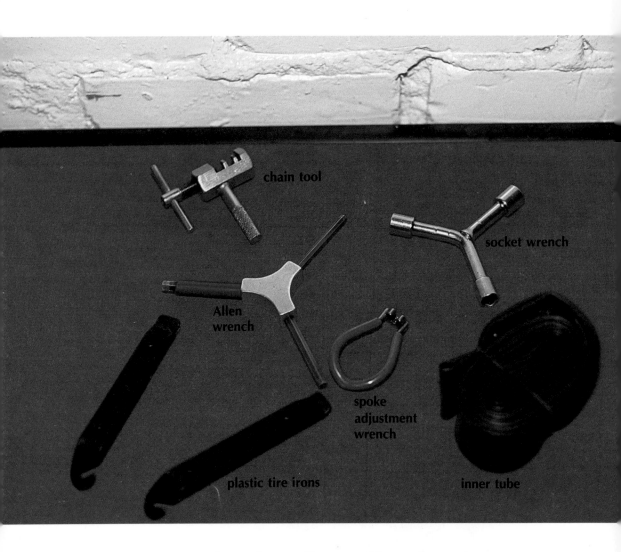

chain tool

socket wrench

Allen wrench

spoke adjustment wrench

plastic tire irons

inner tube

Tools and supplies you'll need on the trail: replacement inner tube, socket wrench, Allen wrench, chain tool, plastic tire irons, and spoke adjustment wrench.

A seat tube pack allows you
to carry your bike on your
shoulder when the
trail is too rough to ride.

shoulder strap. If need be, a shoulder strap can make it easier to carry your bike.

When you return from a ride it is a good idea to wash your bike. Use soap if you can. Get all the mud and sand off the frame and out from in between the sprockets and the chain. Be sure to wipe the bike dry when you are finished so that it will not rust. When you are finished washing and drying the bike, be sure to lubricate the chain.

GETTING THE MOST OUT OF A MOUNTAIN BIKE

One of the keys to having fun riding your mountain bike is to develop endurance. Endurance helps you meet the challenges of the terrain without becoming too tired. The more often you ride, the more endurance you will have and the better your body will be able to meet these challenges. Try to ride different types of terrain for different periods of time. This will get your body used to the variety that mountain biking offers.

Start by riding back roads and trails that are flat. Ride hard one day and rest or ease off a little the next. Start with gentle hill climbs. As your body gets used to the extra effort you need to climb these hills, and as your bike-handling skills improve, you can start climbing steeper hills.

A good riding schedule may include riding flat terrain one day. Ride for a long period and as fast as you can. Then take a shorter ride the next day. On the third day try to climb a lot of hills. Then rest for a day. To avoid the risk of burnout or injury, it is best not to try to ride too much, too far, too fast.

A mountain biker's riding skills are important. Strength alone will not do it. You must be able to pedal, shift, brake, steer and move around, get on and off the seat and over the back tire. Flexing your knees and elbows will also help you keep your mountain bike under control. A mountain biker must know when and how to stand up to get power and traction. A mountain biker must also know when to sit down and be in an **aerodynamic position.** When you are in an aerodynamic position, your mountain bike will roll farther and faster because less wind will be hitting your body.

How you treat your body will also affect how you will be able to handle your bike. Before a long ride, it is a good idea to "fuel up" with foods that are called "carbos" or "carbs" (short for carbohydrates). Carbos include foods such as pasta, and whole grain foods such as whole wheat bread.

Fruits and fresh vegetables are also good sources of energy and nutrition. It is important for a mountain biker to have plenty of water, especially in high altitudes or on hot days, to avoid the danger of dehydration (extreme loss of body fluids).

WHERE TO RIDE A MOUNTAIN BIKE

A mountain bike can go anywhere a ten-speed or BMX bike can go. A mountain bike can also go many places that they cannot. Mountain bikes rank among the most versatile bikes ever made.

You can ride a mountain bike in the city. You will need to follow the same rules other bikes follow. You will also need to wear the same protective gear that other bikers wear in the city.

Pot holes, rocks, bumps, ruts, dirt, dust, and gravel will affect your mountain bike less than a traditional bike. The superior traction and the extra cushion of air that mountain bike tires provide will help smooth out even the roughest paved street. If you find that you ride on paved streets a lot, you can replace your **knobbies** with less aggressive tire treads or even "wide" slicks to help

Learning to ride can
be fun for everyone.

Here's an example of why
mountain bikes are also known
as All-Terrain Bikes.

decrease your rolling resistance on pavement. You will glide farther and be able to go faster with smoother, less knobby mountain bike tires. But, you will find that if you ride off road with them your traction will be greatly reduced.

Many cities and parks have bike paths (a paved area that runs right next to the main road). A mountain bike can handle these areas too.

An excellent place to ride a mountain bike is an empty, grassy field. You can learn how to maneuver your bike over a variety of terrain without having to worry about missing trees and other larger obstacles. After you practice the basic skills of riding off-road you can start riding in areas with trails through the woods. Once you get into a wooded area you will have to be alert for many changes in the terrain including rocks on the trail, low light conditions, stumps, bumps, roots, sand, streams, and just about anything else you can think of that may be found in or near the woods. The same holds true if you ride up and down hills.

If you ride in many different conditions, including pavement, bike paths, gravel roads, paths, trails in the woods, and up and down mountainsides you'll understand the other name for a mountain bike—All-Terrain Bike!

MOUNTAIN BIKE COURTESY AND SAFETY

Because a mountain bike can go almost anywhere, you may share the trails with ATVs (All-Terrain Vehicles), jeeps, and four-wheel-drive vehicles. It is important to be aware of these other vehicles when riding. Always use caution in these areas.

When approaching people riding horses it is important to slow down. Let the riders know that you are approaching. If it is possible, stop and allow the horses and their riders to pass. Always be courteous to other trail users.

Some trails are open to multiple-access use (hikers and bikers). On these trails, keep an eye open for people on the trail. Hikers have the right of way. As with horses, allow hikers plenty of room.

Here is a list of rules published by IMBA (International Mountain Biking Association) for mountain bikers to follow:

1. Ride on trails open to mountain biking.
2. Leave no trace. Do not litter, or throw trash, on the trails, or ride off trails or on closed portions of a trail.

3. Always ride in control. Use caution at all times.
4. Always yield trail to hikers, other mountain bikers, horses, and ATVs.
5. Respect the environment and the animals living in it.
6. Plan ahead. Be aware of other trail users, obstacles, and your abilities whenever and wherever you ride your mountain bike.

There are mountain biking clubs and associations all over the country. These associations often have newsletters and information on where the best places are for mountain biking. They may also be involved in setting up races and competitions and "fun" rides. Mountain bike associations are a good way to enjoy the friendship of other mountain bikers. You can find out about a mountain biking club or association in your area by asking at a bike shop.

MOUNTAIN BIKE RACES, RIDES, AND COMPETITIONS

Mountain bikers can also enjoy racing their mountain bikes. Races take place all over the country, not just in the mountains. There are many

Many ski areas hold
bike races in the summer.

different types of courses. Some are flat, others have lots of hills. A mountain bike racer may encounter sand, mud, rocks, wide **two-track** trails, "single tracks," logs, or other obstacles. This is the major difference between a mountain bike race and a road-race, where riders usually stay on paved roads.

When you ride in a mountain bike race you will usually find that it is a competition between you and the course most of the time. Road racing on a bike usually forms a "pack" of racers who are in the lead. If you don't finish with the pack or in front of it, you may not feel like you are racing.

In an off-road race, the racer can have fun just trying to beat the course. The challenge of the race may be to climb a hill that no one else has been able to climb, or to jump a log that others could not jump. There is always a chance that the trail may prove to be too much even for the leaders. If a part on their bike fails, and they don't finish the race, it will allow you the chance to move up in the standings. Also, unlike road races, it is not always the fastest riders who win. It takes a lot of technical skill just to finish on some off-road courses.

Different races have different classes. You will usually find a class for juniors (fourteen or sev-

**A race course can be a real challenge
for a mountain bike rider.**

enteen and under); a class for beginners; a sport or novice class; and an expert, super pro-, or pro-am class. Girls usually compete against girls in their class. There is usually a class for "vets" (those over thirty-five) and a masters class for those over forty.

Juniors may go around the course once or twice. A junior may ride three or four miles in a race. Beginners may go two or three times around the course. The sport and expert classes may ride twenty miles or more, depending on the race.

MOUNTAIN BIKE COURSES

Mountain bike racing courses are not all the same. Each course is laid out differently—depending on who is in the race, where it is held, and the type of terrain found on the course. Some mountain bike races may take place in a short circle course through the woods. A rider may have to make several laps around the course.

Other courses may be cross-country in design. Cross-country courses have fewer laps, or may only go from one place to another and not make any laps. In either case, racers from one or two classes start together. In small races juniors might even start with the experts. As racers cross the finish line they are separated into their age groups or racing class by the number that they wear on their shirts.

Mountain bikers also compete in time trial events. In a time trial event you must ride from one point (start) to another (finish) in the shortest time. In these events, the course is usually set up so that it takes a lot of skill as well as strength to get a fast time. Riders are started one at a time, at about three-minute intervals, and the one with the fastest time for riding the course wins.

There is also an event called the downhill. A downhill mountain bike course is very similar to a slalom ski racing course. Poles with flags, called gates, are set up in a line down the hill. The mountain biker starts at the top of the hill and must go around each pole or gate from top to bottom. The mountain biker with the fastest time without missing a gate will be the winner. Sometimes the downhill is run on an elimination basis. Two racers start together and the winner in each race moves to the next heat, ending with semifinals and then the final race.

In a hill-climb event, each mountain biker must try to climb the hill as far as he or she can without putting a foot down touching the ground or going

Going around gates in a down- hill race requires a lot of skill.

Young riders may go up smaller hills, but it's still a challenge!

Trials riding is a difficult sport.
You must maneuver the bike up, down,
and around a variety of obstacles.

off the course. Usually, the hill climbing event is held on a hill that is so steep the riders cannot make it to the top. The winner is the one who makes it closest to the top.

Another form of mountain biking is called trials riding. In a trials event the rider must go over several different short courses. Each course has specific obstacles that must be "cleaned" (ridden over without putting a foot down and touching the ground). Every time a rider puts a foot down, he or she receives a point. The rider with the fewest number of points wins.

Trials events, like other mountain biking events, have specific categories for riders of different age groups, sex, and abilities. There is also a separate category for trials bikes. A trials bike has fat tires like a mountain bike. However, it is smaller than a mountain bike, with higher (BMX-style) handlebars and smaller wheels—about twenty inches. It is made to be light and maneuverable, and has very, very low gearing for climbing up short steep obstacles. A trials bike rider must be able to hop the bike; stand still on the bike without pedaling; turn in the air; and generally use the bike as a tool for climbing up, down, and around all sorts of things including rocks, logs, little gullies, short steep hills, and streams.

In mountain bike polo, a player must
be able to brake, shift, and sprint up
and down a field while holding on to
the polo mallet and swinging at the ball.

MOUNTAIN BIKE GAMES

Because a mountain bike is so versatile, mountain bikers have come up with games to play while riding them. Mountain bike polo is one of them. To play mountain bike polo you need enough people on mountain bikes to have two teams of at least four to a side and an empty football or soccer field with a soccer-type goal at each end. Each player has a mallet and there is one ball. You can buy mountain bike polo equipment at a mountain bike shop. An official bicycle polo kit consists of four hardwood mallets, two balls, an official rule book, four goal markers, two goal lines, and a lightweight bag or quiver to carry the gear.

The object is to hit the ball into your goal with the mallet while pedaling, turning, shifting, and braking on your mountain bike. The other team will be trying to block your shots with their mallets and bikes. Most teams play by a set of rules that come with the mountain bike polo equipment, in which bike contact is limited. It is wise to wear protective gear. Many bike shops sponsor teams and compete against one another, organize tournaments, and develop "local" rules.

Mountain bike limbo is a challenge of handling skills. The object is to "limbo" your mountain bike under a pole that is lowered every time someone makes it under the pole. Because a mountain bike is so strong, many competitors pedal toward the limbo pole and then lean against the frame and stretch out to get lower, letting momentum carry them under the pole. It is a tricky maneuver, and it takes a lot of skill to stand up after passing under the pole. If your feet touch the ground while you try to limbo under the pole, you are out of the game.

Shark is a game of balance. In an area about the size of a basketball court, each mountain biker rides around and tries to stop in front of another mountain biker, forcing that biker to stop and put one or both feet down. If a mountain biker puts a foot down he or she is out of the game. You cannot let your feet touch the ground or run into another bike or you will be out of the game also. To be a successful "shark," you have to be able to balance on your bike without moving, hop it around, and steer around and through other stopped or slow-moving bikes.

You can also do the same things you do on any other bike including **wheelies, bunny hops,** and **catching air** on a mountain bike. In fact, practicing

Being able to catch
air and do wheelies
and bunny hops can help
you to handle the trail.

**There are many new types of mountain bikes
to meet the needs of different riders.**

these moves will help you ride better on the trail. Wheelies will help you get over small logs and other obstacles on the trail. Bunny hops will help you get out of tight situations while maintaining your speed. Catching air, whether off a curb or a rise in the trail, shares many of the same skills of balance, bike control, and timing.

"STATE OF THE ART"

In the late 1970s and early 1980s there were only a few hundred mountain bikes in the country. Today they are the hottest selling bikes made. There are hundreds of bicycle companies making millions of mountain bikes. Each year brings new frame designs and new materials that are lighter, stronger, and safer. Many frames now include features such as elevated **chainstays** and over-sized tubing.

Mountain biking components have also come a long way. Early mountain bikes borrowed their brakes, shifters, and tires from other bikes such as ten-speeds, BMX bikes, and moto-cross motorcycles. Today the components found on mountain bikes are made for mountain biking. Most include fifteen, eighteen, or twenty-one speeds with index shifting, which allows the rider to shift up or down by pushing the shift handle up or down one notch or "click." To help keep the rider's hands on the bars, shifting systems are now being mounted underneath the handle bars instead of on top, so that the rider can shift to the next gear by using just the thumb.

There are now a variety of different tire tread designs. Some tires are made of kevlar, a very light and strong material. There are brake levers, cables, water bottle cages, tire pumps, riding lights, handle bars, stems, seats, bike racks, and other components that are designed just for mountain bikes. Each year mountain bikes are lighter, stronger, faster, and safer than ever before.

Today almost all bicycle companies have mountain bike race teams. They compete in races not only in northern California, but all over the United States, Canada, and Europe. This provides a variety of conditions and terrains. These races and riders give bicycle companies the opportunity to test new equipment and designs.

The future of mountain biking is exciting. As new mountain bikes and components hit the market, new trails and events are opening up all over the country. A mountain bike gives the rider the opportunity to go just about anywhere he or she

The trail beckons. . . .

wants to, from back and forth to school, deep into the woods, up hills, to the top of some of the highest mountains. The question that every mountain biker likes to be asked is, "Where would you like to ride next?"

GLOSSARY

Aerodynamic position: The position the rider takes on the bike in order to let air flow over and around the body with as little interference as possible.

Bottom bracket height: The distance from the ground to the center of the crank spindle. Low bottom brackets lend stability; high bottom brackets yield cornering clearance and ground clearance.

Bunny hop: Jumping the mountain bike off the ground. Being able to bunny hop can help a mountain bike rider clear obstacles in the trail such as rocks, stumps, logs, and ruts.

Catching air: When a mountain biker hits a rise or small drop-off in the trail, the bike and rider may be in the air momentarily. When landing, the rider must be careful to keep the bike balanced and avoid landing off the trail.

Chainring: The rings (attached to the crank arms) that the chain rides on. The chainrings are turned by the pedals. A mountain bike can have as many as four chainrings.

Chainstay: The length of tube(s) that connect the bottom bracket to the rear axle.

Crank set: Includes the pedals, chainrings, and bottom bracket of the bike.

Derailleur: The device that moves the chain up or down on the chainrings (the front derailleur), or up and down on the sprockets connected to the rear wheel (rear derailleur).

Foot straps: A plastic or metal band with a strap attached that secures the foot to the pedal for more power and better control.

Freewheel: A device attached to the rear wheel of a bicycle, permitting wheel motion without pedal action, as in coasting. A mountain bike can have as many as eight cogs on the freewheel, which allows the rider a wide range of gear choices.

Knobbies: Mountain bike tires with aggressive tread pattern.

Quick release: A device that allows for fast adjustment or release of the seat or wheels.

Shorty levers (two-finger levers): The shape of a brake lever. They are shorter than traditional levers. This is so they are less likely to snag or get caught on something while riding down a trail.

Stand-over height: Refers to the room a bicyclist has when standing over the top tube of the bike. A mountain biker should allow about three inches of clearance between the top tube of the bike and the crotch area.

Two-track: A trail wide enough for two or more bikers to ride abreast.

Wheelbase: The measurement between the front and rear axles, center to center. A long wheelbase measurement can make a bike ride smoother; a short wheelbase measurement can make a bike respond quicker in terms of turning and handling.

FOR FURTHER READING

For more information on mountain bikes and mountain biking:

All-Terrain Bikes, by the editors of *Bicycling Magazine.* Emmaus, PA.: Rodale Press, 1985.

Bicycling Magazine, Rodale Press, Inc., 33 E. Minor Street, Emmaus, PA 18098.

Cyclist Magazine, P.O. Box 53925, Boulder, CO 80322-3925.

Mountain Bike Action Magazine, Daisy/Hi-Torque Publishing Company, Inc., 10600 Sepulveda Boulevard, Mission Hills, CA 91354.

Mountain Bike Magazine, Rodale Press, Inc., 33 E. Minor Street, Emmaus, PA 18098.

Mountain & City Biking Magazine, Challenge Publications Inc., 7950 Deering Ave., Canoga Park, CA 91304.

INDEX

ABOUT THE AUTHOR

A resident of Michigan, Dwain Abramowski is a mountain biking enthusiast and currently the editor of the *Bent Rim Bugle*, a local mountain biking magazine. He has also worked as an early-childhood teacher. Mr. Abramowski also writes a column called "Young Minds," on issues of interest to parents and their children, for his local newspaper. He is married and has one son.